Memories to Cherish

The cast of "The Magic Toy Shop" dedicates this book to all of you who, once upon a time,

put your thumbs at the corners of your mouths and came through that magic door to join

us, and to the memory of GORDON ALDERMAN, who brought all of us together and

ELIZABETH WILSON DAUGHERTY ("Mrs. Dee"), who earned the title "Mother Superior"

of "The Magic Toy Shop" by sharing songs, stories, philosophy and love, and to

THE STAFF OF THE ONONDAGA HISTORICAL ASSOCIATION for recognizing that

childhood memories and a more recent past are an important part of our history.

ISBN 0-9654732-2-8

LIMITED EDITION

Book Number

Introduction

The Onondaga Historical Association (OHA) serves as trustee of this community's major public history museum and research center in downtown Syracuse. OHA is committed to projects that will increase the understanding, appreciation, interpretation, sharing and enjoyment of the history and traditions of Onondaga County and its residents.

This year of 1998, the City of Syracuse celebrates its sesquicentennial. This year also marks the 50th anniversary of television's arrival in our community. On December 1, 1948, station WHEN (now WTVH-5) transmitted Syracuse's first regular broadcast of a TV program from its pioneering studio at 101 Court Street. On that historic day, no one could have imagined the influence this new medium would have on our lives.

Few programs had more lasting impact than "The Magic Toy Shop," one of local television's most endearing, recognized and long-standing productions. This show played a significant role in the lives of countless Central New Yorkers for nearly 30 years. It is now a treasured part of Onondaga County's rich heritage. The dream of creating a permanent home for the legacy of "The Magic Toy Shop" was born in 1989 when OHA hosted a one-time holiday exhibit about the program. OHA discovered how many museum visitors wanted to be able to keep their childhood memories alive and also allow their children the opportunity to experience the gentler world of an earlier time.

This limited edition book was published in celebration of local television's 50th anniversary and to raise funds to install a permanent exhibit on "The Magic Toy Shop" and its era. This exhibit will be one designed to build a bond between generations, to spur imagination with interesting and creative activities, to explore our more recent past, and to help attract people to downtown Syracuse where there is a whole world to discover both in and outside the OHA Museum.

The Onondaga Historical Association hopes that you enjoy this book and, with appreciation to all of its many supporters, wishes to especially thank the following major underwriters and sponsors.

The John Ben Snow Foundation
Ralph & Renate BeVard
KeyBank
Lockheed Martin Corporation
New York State Tourism Grant Program Supported by
State Senator John DeFrancisco
Bristol-Myers Squibb Company
Horace J. Landry
The Frank & Frances Revoir Foundation
Syroco, Inc.
The Ridings Foundation, Inc.
WTVH-5, Granite Broadcasting Corporation

From the first edition of the Festival of Nations, "Magic Toy Shop" welcomed young performers.

The Alderman Sisters were regular guest stars.

Youngsters earned applause in talent shows.

1955

— It was a very good year. Dwight Eisenhower was president. W. Averell Harriman was governor of New York. Donald Meade was mayor of Syracuse. It was the era of the "Baby Boomers." Prices were low. McDonald's introduced its first hamburger. The cost was 15 cents.

On the sports scene, the Syracuse Nats were NBA champions; the Brooklyn Dodgers won their first and only World Series.

People were singing "Love and Marriage," written by Syracuse's own Jimmy Van Heusen.

In California, Disneyland opened and was billed as "the happiest place on earth."

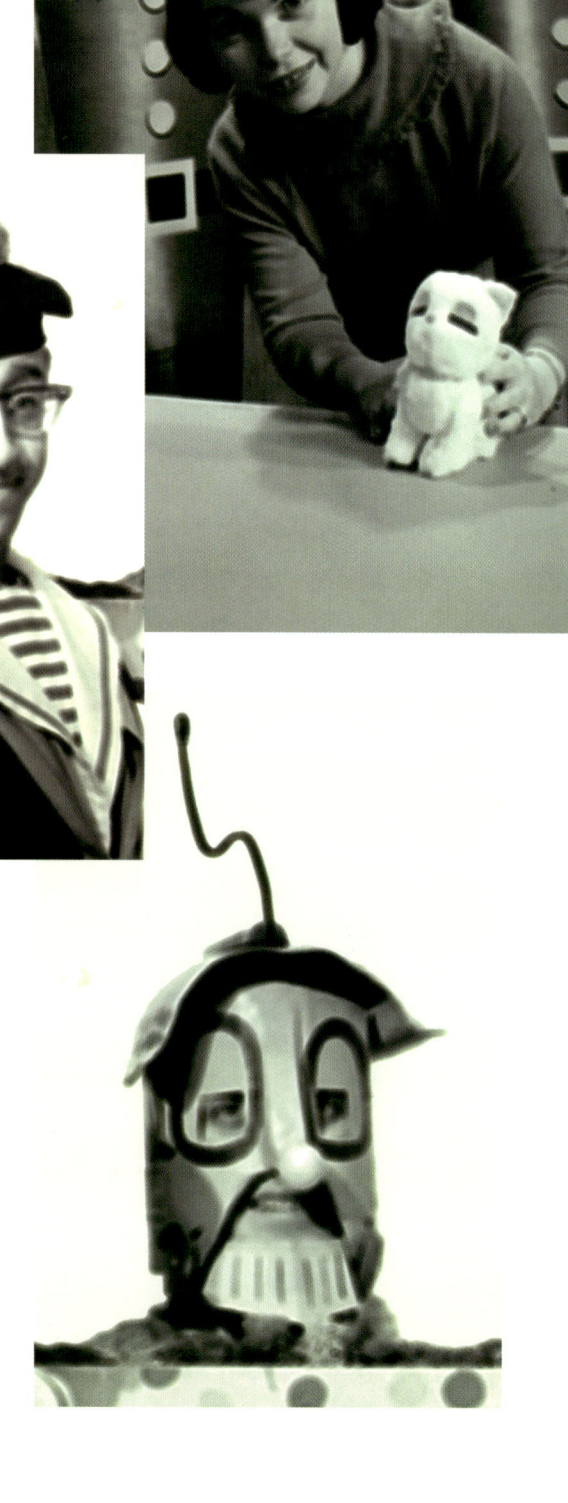

And on February 28 of the year 1955, Central New York children first put their thumbs at the corners of their mouths, turned them up into a smile and walked through the door of "The Magic Toy Shop." Their entrance signaled the important time in their young lives when they met the cast members who would become part of their childhood:

Merrily — always introduced as the "pretty proprietress of the Magic Toy Shop."

Eddie Flum Num — her chief assistant and an artist who created all the sets and drew the stories told by Mr. Trolley.

Mr. Trolley — known as the best storyteller in the whole world and outer space, who also brought news from beyond the Magic Door.

Twinkle — a cousin to all clowns, who talked only in music so children would learn to listen.

Toward the end of that first year, the Play Lady was introduced. A grandmother figure, she appeared from Toyland whenever they needed her. She brought to the Toy Shop two prized possessions — The Flum-o-matic projector (designed by and named for Eddie Flum Num) that would show only movies that boys and girls liked; and the Abracadabra Book that allowed them to travel any time, to any place.

The "Magic" of the Toy Shop was from the toys themselves, who came to life at night. "Floogie" was the general of all the toys, named for his gentle but firm treatment of the others. "Tommy Pup Dog" was always tired. (It was reported that he taught dancing at night.)

The toys, through Merrily, sent messages to the boys and girls urging them to be kind to the toys in their own homes and to everyone they met.

When "Magic Toy Shop" made its debut, television in Central New York was only 6 years and 3 months old. On December 1, 1948, WHEN-Channel 8 (now WTVH-Channel 5) signed on the air and life was never really the same again.

On the station's fifth birthday in 1953, General Manager Paul Adanti announced that the next project would be a quality program for children. Program Director Gordon Alderman selected Jean Daugherty to write and produce a pilot. At the same time, he recruited experts in early childhood training to act as an advisory committee. Representatives from mothers' clubs, PTAs, the Syracuse city schools, Syracuse University, SUNY Oswego and the Syracuse Public Library met and determined that these adults could decide what children should watch — but in the end, it was the children who decided what they would watch.

The adult organization reps selected test families to watch the pilot in their own homes. Using a questionnaire devised for them by Syracuse University researcher Lawrence Myers, parents recorded their reactions and suggestions and those of their children.

The story's original proprietor was a character named Mr. Fudge. He reminded the children too much of Santa Claus, and that role eventually became the "Merrily" part.

The station spent over a year in polishings, but in the meantime, a summer series, "Tip Top Showboat," was produced, featuring Captain Bob and Rusty, Eddie Flum Num and First Mate Mike. For the first time, children heard Mr. Trolley's stories.

Children became part of the studio audience, making their way to the studios of WHEN, then located in a former factory at 101 Court Street on Syracuse's north side; and as the young visitors were asked to name their favorite section of the show, they gave a two thumbs up to that dynamic duo, Mr. Trolley and Eddie Flum Num. That same summer, a newcomer to the station staff, Marylin Hubbard Herr, was chosen to host an afternoon show called "Merrily's Magic Music Box," featuring RCA Reader Record Albums. Children again gave a stamp of approval.

Finally, the show went into production. There were never auditions for "Magic Toy Shop." The five cast members were all working at WHEN in different jobs.

Merrily (Marylin Hubbard Herr) was in the program department. She brought special skills to her role. She had studied at the American Academy in New York and had toured with Clare Tree Major's Children's Theater. She also earned a degree from Syracuse University.

Eddie Flum Num (Socrates Sampson), a graduate of Syracuse University, was the station's art director, responsible for everything from set design to visuals for commercials.

At the station, Lewis B. O'Donnell held the title, "sales service coordinator." Another Syracuse alumnus (he eventually earned a master's and a Ph.D.), Lew had the difficult assignment of creating a character using his voice, his eyes and a nose that lit up, for it was Paul Adanti's one mandate that the show have a trolley car. The station manager had no idea what that character should look like, but Lew evidently filled the bill.

Twinkle (Tony Riposo) was musical director at WHEN. A graduate of S.U.'s School of Music, he was an accomplished musician, composer and arranger.

Jean Daugherty, an assistant to the program director responsible for writing and producing documentaries, called her "Magic Toy Shop" assignment the "icing on the cake."

She, too, held an S.U. degree. Jean eventually had to relinquish her job as director to become "Toy Shop's" Play Lady.

There were those who said, "What luck that these five people should be in the same place at the same time." But Marylin always thought the cast was part of a puzzle just waiting to be put together.

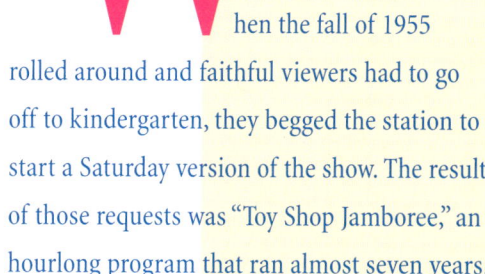

When the fall of 1955 rolled around and faithful viewers had to go off to kindergarten, they begged the station to start a Saturday version of the show. The result of those requests was "Toy Shop Jamboree," an hourlong program that ran almost seven years.

Gordon Alderman and Lew O'Donnell joined the cast as song and dance men. (Lew did double duty as Mr. Trolley.) Each show had a theme, and busier-than-ever Socrates Sampson created new sets each week.

Children were introduced to songs from Broadway and movies; young performers were guest stars; but best of all, the show included a studio audience. Youngsters participated on the air — and always shared a postshow party with the cast.

T he cast also "hit the road":

They were "live" at the State Fair…

They were at places like Suburban Park.

They often shared the stage with their good friend "Uncle Skip" (John Scott), host of "Cartoon Clubhouse."

They played schools, church basements, did benefit performances…
Nothing brought greater joy than meeting fans in person.

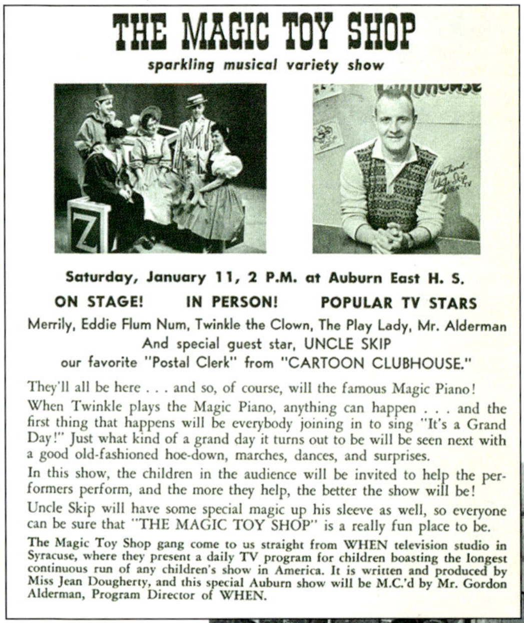

THE MAGIC TOY SHOP
sparkling musical variety show

Saturday, January 11, 2 P.M. at Auburn East H. S.
ON STAGE!   IN PERSON!   POPULAR TV STARS
Merrily, Eddie Flum Num, Twinkle the Clown, The Play Lady, Mr. Alderman
And special guest star, UNCLE SKIP
our favorite "Postal Clerk" from "CARTOON CLUBHOUSE."

They'll all be here . . . and so, of course, will the famous Magic Piano!
When Twinkle plays the Magic Piano, anything can happen . . . and the first thing that happens will be everybody joining in to sing "It's a Grand Day!" Just what kind of a grand day it turns out to be will be seen next with a good old-fashioned hoe-down, marches, dances, and surprises.
In this show, the children in the audience will be invited to help the performers perform, and the more they help, the better the show will be!
Uncle Skip will have some special magic up his sleeve as well, so everyone can be sure that "THE MAGIC TOY SHOP" is a really fun place to be.
The Magic Toy Shop gang come to us straight from WHEN television studio in Syracuse, where they present a daily TV program for children boasting the longest continuous run of any children's show in America. It is written and produced by Miss Jean Dougherty, and this special Auburn show will be M.C.'d by Mr. Gordon Alderman, Program Director of WHEN.

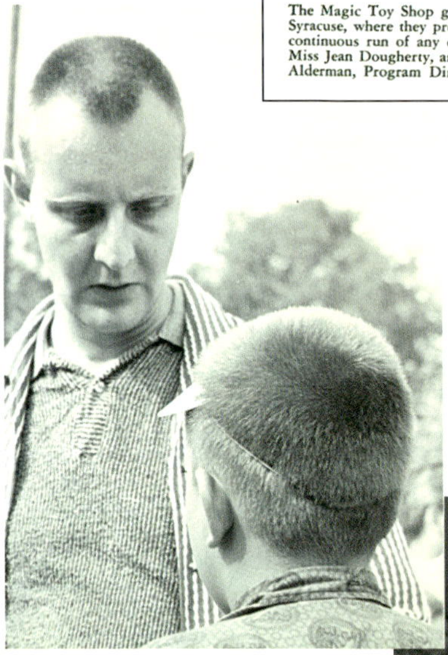

T

here were special projects, too… and none more meaningful than the gift they received on "Magic Toy Shop's" fifth birthday when the station decided to sponsor a foster child from Korea. Park Myung Hi and her family were "pen pals" and Central New York children discovered that half a world away, other children were very much like them. Because of this, and because Christmas gifts had to be sent months ahead, the show's "Christmas in July" segment became an important celebration.

STORY OF MAGIC TOY SHOP'S 'PARENTHOOD'

A Feature Report
By Shirley Baum

How do you explain to a little child who lives in poverty, and who has never seen or heard of a TV set, that her new Foster Parents are the cast and audience of a television show? Park Myung Hi, the Korean Foster Child adopted by WHEN-TV's "Magic Toy Shop," thought her Foster Parents were fairy godmothers and magicians who spent each day dispensing toys and magic to children. This enchanting thought was not entirely dispelled when she saw her first television program.

Park Myung Hi lives in her maternal uncle's home on the outskirts of Seoul, South Korea with her mother, her elder brother Myung Sam and her two little sisters Myung Sim and Myung Ae. The family had fled their home in North Korea and, with the death of their father, they were left destitute. Their uncle earned barely enough to feed and clothe his own family so Mrs. Park was forced to seek work. Until illness struck, the mother peddled vegetables carrying the youngest child on her back while she worked. This labor brought in about 30c a day and provided for a bare subsistence with no money left over for clothing and school supplies.

To this despairing family, the "Magic Toy Shop" offered some very real magic. Four years ago, WHEN-TV, through the Foster Parents Plan, a non-profit organization designed to help needy children throughout the world, requested an opportunity to become the Foster Parents of a Korean child. It was felt that the Korean culture would provide more varied interest for the program enjoys more each year of its foster parenthood.

The letters written by the children and Mrs. Park reflect the charming oriental appreciation of beauty and never fail to express their gratitude to their benefactors. In one of her letters Park Myung Hi said, "Due to your love and care, I and my elder brother study without any troubles.

Her mother peddled vegetables for 30c a day while carrying her youngest on her back. That's only part of the story of Park Myung Hi, "The Magic Toy Shop" Korean Foster Parents Child adopted by the program and WHEN-TV four years ago. A recent photo against the setting of an actual letter from Myung Hi shows a very happy youngster in the fourth grade of primary school.

delight of all the Park family, a globe of the world.

We at WHEN-TV are very proud of our industrious Korean family and our lives are being enriched by our association with Mrs. Park and her four children. To quote Myung Hi, "… it is good for our futures."

Behind the Scenes

"**M**agic Toy Shop" was born in the days of live television — no videotapes, no second chance, no opportunity to store episodes for vacation time — so temporary replacements were built into the format.

Merrily could always summon the Play Lady.

Eddie Flum Num boasted a family of six brothers. All had the first name "Eddie" and the family name "Num"; each had a different middle name. For instance, Eddie Sum Num was good at math; Eddie Hum Num liked to sing. "Flum" is a word that means "very good." Since this particular Eddie was a very good artist, he earned that title. Only Eddie Crumb Num, a brother who always carried peanut butter crackers in his pocket, appeared on the show. There was also Eddie Mum Num, who could keep a secret; Eddie Tum Num, who liked to eat; and Eddie Drum Num, who was a great percussionist.

Mr. Trolley had two relatives he could call on — his wife, "Mignonette," and his cousin "Texas Trolley."

When Twinkle went on vacation, children said a special phrase and turned an ordinary piano into a magic one that played by itself. Off the set, some of the area's finest musicians filled in for the talented Tony Riposo. In the summer of 1955, Mario DeSantis became the first Magic Piano and continued for the duration of the show.
He called most often on Joe Carfagno and Sox Tiffault.

Do you know who's who in the Num clan?

Birthdays were a cause for celebration. The show's 10th birthday in 1965 was celebrated for an entire week. By that time, WHEN had moved to new headquarters at 980 James St. In 1963, the "Magic Toy Shop" had the honor of being the first broadcast in the new building.

The scope of the program continued to expand. There were trips on the Abracadabra Book and lessons from swimming, to skiing, to skating.

But most importantly, there was fun…

The 1970s brought more changes. Tony Riposo, who had been traveling with the McGuire Sisters, decided to make the career move permanent and he sent his cousin Maestro to take over. Maestro's touch at the piano was very much like that of the original "Magic Piano," Mario DeSantis.

In 1972, the first new cast member became a regular guest. Eleanor Russell's childhood dream had been to be "on the 'Magic Toy Shop,' not as a member of a studio audience but as a performer." One of the founders of the "Soul Generation," Eleanor invited children to "Ellie's Place," where she shared songs and stories.

In 1976 came the biggest changes of all — WHEN became WTVH and "Magic Toy Shop" became "Toy Shop Corporation," an hourlong program that aired Saturdays and Sundays.

18

Merrily was president of the Corporation...

Eddie Flum Num ran a shop called Y.N.I.W.H.I. (You Need It We Have It)...

Lew O'Donnell played Aloysius Alonzo Barnaby Brown, an expediter...

Mario DeSantis, not surprisingly, was in charge of the music shop...

Ellie reported on entertainment news and presented teen performers...

The Play Lady welcomed people to a travel agency. Her chief assistant was a butterfly named Melissa...

The Bookworms provided book reviews. Their voices sounded like those of Socrates Sampson and Betty Ann Kram...

The program itself provided a showcase for teen talent...

And, in a special series called "Central New York Makes It," young viewers were given a look at businesses in their community.

This band of young men from Syracuse showcased their talent at the State Fair.

Sheila Skipworth performed numbers from Broadway shows such as "The Wiz."

Mr. Ralph BeVard of The Eraser Company explains the workings of his plant to the young viewers of "Toy Shop Corporation."

Each week, a young person was named a VSP, a Very Special Person, and received a plaque.

In September 1982, the cast said final goodbyes, but the memories will go on for a lifetime — because, to quote Merrily: "We are forever friends."

22

This is the original theme music for "The Magic Toy Shop." Little did composer Tony Riposo (Twinkle) realize that it would become one of the best known melodies in Central New York. The tattered copy seen here was used by Twinkle and the Magic Pianos for the duration of the show. It truly is a part of history.

For all of us who were part of "Magic Toy Shop," it was more than a TV program. It was a chance to light up the lives of children, to help them use their imagination, to encourage them to believe in themselves, and perhaps most important of all, to realize how lucky we are to live in a community where diversity blends us into a beautiful mosaic. If schools were established to teach the three R's, we existed to teach the fourth — Respect.

We used music, art, field trips — even the toys became teachers. But undoubtedly, story time gave us the greatest opportunities. Those of you who first turned on a smile will remember Mr. Trolley, known as the best storyteller in the whole world and outer space. Lew O'Donnell, who created the role, had a boundless range of voices that brought life to stories especially written for "Magic Toy Shop." As the author, I admit that they subtly but unabashedly taught a lesson. The music of Twinkle (Tony Riposo) enhanced them, however, we all depended on a kind of magician with a grease pencil to bring them to life. That was Eddie Flum Num, of course, the super talented Socrates Sampson, who fascinated children and adults alike by turning abstract shapes into characters on a page.

Perhaps we had a sense of history or perhaps we couldn't let go of our past. Whatever the reason, the original storyboards were preserved and the illustrations for this book are the original drawings — in a very real way a gift from Socrates Sampson.

We can't provide the voice of Mr. Trolley or the wonderful background music of Twinkle, but we're hoping that grown-ups will be sharing these stories with another generation and that all of you will enjoy meeting (either again, or for the first time) the colorful characters who were part of a kinder, gentler age. We also hope that you'll recapture that age when the permanent exhibit of "The Magic Toy Shop" opens and you know that your purchase of this book helped make the exhibit possible.

This was the first story we shared with viewers in 1955. It remained a favorite — that was understandable because even in an age of electronic marvels, the teddy bear still holds a special spot in the hearts of children.

How the Teddy Bear Got His Name

Story written by Jean Daugherty and illustrated by Socrates Sampson.

This is partly a make-believe story and partly a true story, all about how the Teddy Bear got its name. This was a long time ago when your mother's grandmother was a little girl and the story takes place in a big woods, a beautiful, big woods with big trees and little trees, flowers and birds.

Into this woods one day came a big hunter. He had a checked coat — it looked just like a checkerboard, and he had a great, great big gun. Now this big hunter wasn't afraid of anything. No indeed, he wasn't. He was the bravest hunter in the whole world. He wasn't afraid of lions. The biggest, fiercest lion didn't scare him a bit because he was the bravest hunter in the whole wide world. He wasn't afraid of deer. Not even the king of the whole herd who had big, sharp horns. He wasn't afraid because he was the bravest hunter in all the world. He wasn't afraid of elephants, either. Not giant elephants with giant trunks. Truly, he was a brave hunter.

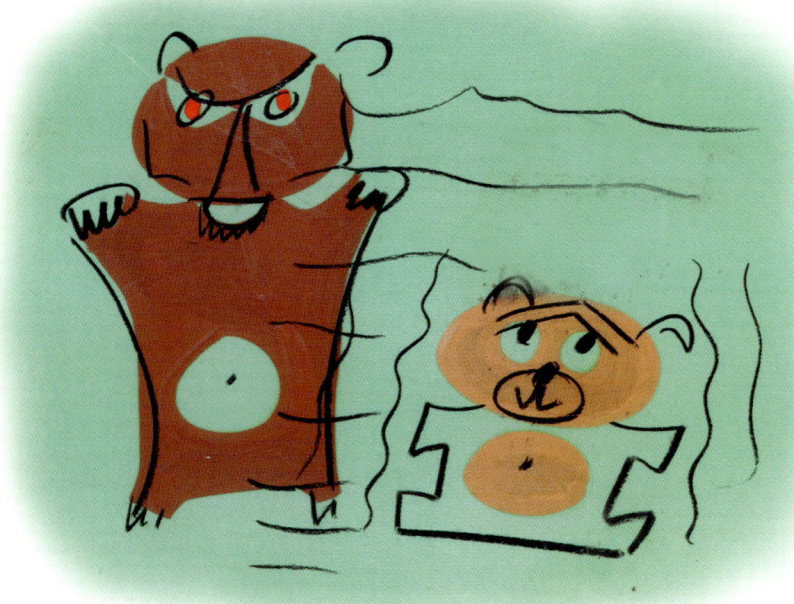

Well, this day in the woods he saw a bear, a grizzly bear with big teeth, coming right toward him. Well, the brave hunter lifted his gun to shoot. When he did, he noticed that in between the grizzly bear and himself was a little cub. The brave hunter couldn't shoot him. He couldn't take a chance on hitting the baby bear. He didn't need to worry about the gun, because as soon as the grizzly bear saw that this hunter was the bravest in the world, he ran back into the woods and hid among the big trees and little trees and the flowers and birds.

But the little bear cub was afraid to run away. He just stood where he was and quivered and shivered and shivered and quivered until the big brave hunter walked right up to the little bear and said, "Don't cry, little bear, I won't hurt you. Truly, I won't." And the little bear looked right into the big hunter's eyes and he knew this was so. Here was a kind, kind man. Then the big, brave hunter said, "What's your name, little bear?" And the little bear started to cry.

So the hunter said, "Mercy me, little bear, there's no reason to cry. All I said was what's your name?" And the little bear cried harder than ever. So the hunter said, "Come, come now, tell me what's the matter."

"Well, you see, sir," answered the little bear, "I don't have a name. My mother and father were taken off to a zoo when I was very small, before they'd even had a chance to give me a name. Now all the other bears call me 'hey.'" Then he started to cry. "I don't want to be a 'Hey Bear.' I want to have a name." "Now, dry those tears," said the brave hunter. "I have a name that's big enough for both of us. I'll let you use mine."

"What is your name, sir?" said the little bear. "At the White House where I live, they call me Mr. Roosevelt, but my friends just call me Teddy and that's what your name will be. Teddy, Teddy Bear." And from that day to this, little bears have been called "Teddy."

Every child, it seems, wants to grow up in a hurry and hates being the smallest. This is the story of one little boy whose dream came true.

The Smallest in the Family

It really was a very big name for a little boy, Timothy Aloysius Donovan the Third. Maybe that's why nobody ever called him that. His mother and father, grandmother and grandfather and assorted aunts and uncles had started to call him Timmy. Then his cousins nicknamed him "Tad" because, they explained, if you took the T from Timothy, the A from Aloysius and the D from Donovan, you got T-A-D and because he was the youngest and the smallest in the family, they decided that Tadpole was just the right name for a very little cousin.

Timothy Aloysius didn't mind being called "Tad." Really and truly he didn't. But when the cousins called him Tadpole, he knew that the next thing they were going to say was "You're much too little to play this game" or "You can't go with us, Tadpole, you're the smallest in the family" and he was. Even Tad had to admit that. Everybody, everybody was bigger than he was. Even his cousin Susan Marie and she was a girl.

Tad tried to catch up. He ate all his vegetables and he drank his milk every day. His mother tried to explain, "They have a head start. They're older than you." But Tad just said, "I'll catch up. I don't want to be the smallest. I'll be Tad but I won't be Tadpole." And he reached for more milk.

And he did grow, but so did his cousins. He just couldn't run as fast or jump as high as they could. Sometimes they let him tag along, but when he put on his genuine imitation African hunter's helmet and tried to join them on the long hike they called a safari, they said, "We want you to come, Tadpole, really we do, but you can't keep up. You're too little." He couldn't help crying as he watched them leave. "I don't want to be the smallest," he sobbed. His mother said quietly, "Just be patient, Tad, I promise you you won't always be the smallest."

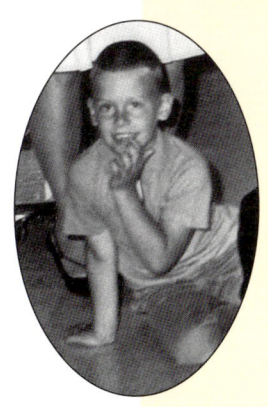

His mother, as always, told the truth. One week Tad went to visit Grammy Donovan. When he got home, there was a surprise. Tad and his father tiptoed into the bedroom. There was a basket there. A basket his father called a bassinet. His father told him to look inside. Tad did and there was a tiny baby. Oh a very tiny baby, much, much, much smaller than Tad. "That's your new brother," his father said, "Thomas Andrew Donovan." "He's in the family," said Tad in such a loud voice that his mother started to shush him. But he was so excited she didn't have the heart to tell him to be quiet. "He's the smallest in the family. He's Tadpole and I'm. . .I'm his big brother!"

And Tad is a very good big brother. The baby is growing. He's walking now, but of course, he's not nearly as big as Tad. Tad teaches him many things and shares most of his toys and it's only once in a while that he looks down at him and says, "You can't do that, Tadpole, you're too little. You're the smallest in the family."

"Everyone has a talent and an obligation to develop it" — That's what my mother, who inspired these stories, told us. Katie Hippopotamus worked hard to find her place in the spotlight. Dreams are important, but working to make them come true is even more important.

Katie Hippopotamus

Katie Hippopotamus was a part of the circus. She had her own special cage in the animal tent. The boys and girls all came to see her. They smiled at Katie and she smiled back. But really and truly she wasn't happy. She didn't want to be in the animal tent. She wanted to be under the Big Top; Katie Hippopotamus wanted to be a star! So the circus owner decided to give her a chance.

Katie had dreamed of being the Hippopotamus on the Flying Trapeze; so they let her try it. Katie didn't like to admit it, but the swinging made her dizzy. She would never be a success on the trapeze. She would just have to think of something else.

So Katie decided to be a tightrope walker. The other stars told her all they knew...the owner gave her an umbrella to help keep her balance, but Katie Hippopotamus was so heavy that when she got on the tightrope it sagged. She wasn't walking high over the heads of people. She was right in the middle of them. This would never do. So the circus owner let Katie try playing in the band.

He gave her a flute. He was sure that everyone would notice the biggest animal in the band playing the smallest instrument. Katie would certainly be a star in no time at all. But Katie, even when she blew with all her might, couldn't make music come out of the flute. By this time she was really discouraged.

Katie was almost in tears that day when she talked to her friend, Elly Elephant. "I might as well give up and go back to the animal tent," Katie sobbed. "I'll never be a star." "Don't give up," said Elly. "We'll think of something. It will have to be something unusual. Something no other animal can do." Just then two boys shouted "hello" as they went past the animals. They looked as though they were flying, but they weren't flying at all. They were roller-skating. "Look at them," shouted Elly Elephant, "there's your answer, Katie."

And it was the answer. Katie Hippopotamus bought a special pair of skates; she practiced night and day, day and night. When the circus opened in the biggest city in the country, the people saw her act for the first time…They cheered and cheered. Katie was a star! Now everyone rushed to the circus to see Katie the Skating Hippopotamus. She's really happy. When anyone asks her advice about becoming a star, Katie says, "First of all you have to find the thing that's right for you…" The trapeze artists, the tightrope walkers, the animals in the band, all nod in agreement as Katie skates by.

A lot of us have the same problem as "Wait-a-While" O'Hara. We tend to put things off. This story has his grandfather practicing "tough love" to help change the boy's bad habit.

Wait-a-While O'Hara

Once upon a time, and I must admit the time is right here and now, there was a little boy named "Wait-a-While O'Hara." Of course, that wasn't his real name. He had a perfectly ordinary name, Timothy Shawn O'Hara. But everybody called him Wait-a-While. Everybody from his grandfather to his very smallest cousin and there was a very good reason why they did. You see, Wait-a-While O'Hara never, never wanted to do things when he was asked to.

"Timothy Shawn O'Hara," his mother called, "will you please come to lunch right now?" When his mother said "Timothy Shawn" in that particular tone, he knew she meant business. But he called back, "Wait a while, Mother, I'll be there in a minute, but I'm right in the middle of a very important project." It seems that Timothy Shawn was always smack in the middle of an important project. He said, "wait a while" when his friends wanted him to play. He said it at breakfast time and bedtime, too. "Wait a while, wait a while, wait a while."

Then one day, his grandfather took him aside. "Wait-a-While," he said seriously, "one of these days, you're going to wait too long. You'll miss something very important and you'll be sorry." "I do mean to hurry, Grandpa," said Wait-a-While, "and I'm going to try to hurry. I'm going to try very hard." "I'll help you," said Grandpa. "From now on, I'll call you just once. That's all, and if you decide to wait a while, you'll wait alone." And Grandpa kept his word.

That very next Saturday, he invited Wait-a-While and his sister, Jennifer, and his little cousins, Terry and Lizabeth, to go to the amusement park. Grandpa told them just exactly when to get ready and they were all set to go, all except Timothy Shawn. He was in the middle of a big project.

"Wait a while, Grandpa," he said. "I'll be ready in a minute." But Grandpa didn't wait. He opened the door. Jennifer, Terry and Lizabeth all climbed in and off they went. Just as Grandpa had predicted, Wait-a-While was waiting all alone!

That was the most miserable afternoon that Timothy Shawn had ever spent. The most miserable and the longest. The minutes dragged. He couldn't even remember what project had kept him so busy. All he could think of was the fun the others must be having at the amusement park. He was absolutely, positively sure that they would ride the Ferris wheel, and there was nothing Timothy Shawn enjoyed quite as much as a ride on the Ferris wheel, unless it might be two rides. But he'd waited too long. "I'll never say wait a while again," he said.

Well, of course, he did say it again many times. But he tried not to say it. And the day finally came when he reserved it for only extra, extra special projects. In fact, he said it so seldom that people began to forget that he'd ever been called "Wait-a-While." He was always first at the breakfast table, first in line at school. So when a band started, it was only natural that the boy out in front should be Timothy Shawn. So the next time you see a band go marching by, take a good look at the drum major. It may be "Speed" O'Hara, the fellow they used to call "Wait-a-While."

Jennifer thought she was a failure, but by doing a kind deed for a lonely scarecrow, she changed the look of Halloween.

The Little Witch

Jennifer was a witch...a very little witch. In fact, she was the very youngest student at the school for witches and it can honestly be said that she wasn't a very good pupil. You see, Jennifer was always happy, and no matter how many times the teachers told her that witches were supposed to be mean and mysterious, Jennifer just could not put on a frown. The professor in charge of gloomy looks finally threw up her hands and said, "She's always going to look happy, but maybe she'll be an expert in some other field."

That's why Jennifer got transferred to the cooking class. She was to learn to make witches' brew...the most bitter concoction in the whole world. Jennifer Witch tried to be successful, she really did, but when the teacher tasted it, she exclaimed, "Oh, this is awful"... "What's the matter with it?" asked Jennifer. "It's delicious," said the teacher. "It's onion soup," said Jennifer proudly. "It is," said the teacher and fainted dead away. Never, never in all the history of the school had a witch made a brew that tasted good!

Jennifer was really in trouble after that. She was sent to the principal's office. She repeated her vow of witchhood once again, "I hereby promise to haunt and frighten, to cast spells and generally cause trouble" and the next week on Halloween, Jennifer started off on her broomstick determined to make good. She was going to be so fierce that just the mention of her name would cause people to tremble. Jennifer looked down out of the skies and saw a scarecrow. That was certainly a good place to start her new career. A scarecrow scared crows and if she scared a scarecrow, she would surely be a success…so down she zoomed.

And nobody, but nobody, was more surprised than Jennifer when the scarecrow said, "Hi." "Aren't you afraid of me?" asked Jennifer. "I'm glad to see you," said the scarecrow. "It's very lonesome here. I'm so terrible looking that the crows never come near and it's no fun at all to stay here all by myself. It makes me cry just to think of it." Well, if there was anything Jennifer couldn't stand, it was tears. "Stop crying," she said to the scarecrow. "I'll find someone to keep you company."

Jennifer looked around and saw a pumpkin in the field. Now really and truly he didn't look like much company, but Jennifer had a plan. She would cast a spell and make the pumpkin into a person. She said a few abracadabras, tossed in a presto change-o, and right before the very eyes of the scarecrow, that pumpkin became a Jack-O-Lantern. . .the happiest, friendliest Jack-O-Lantern that ever lived. "There, Mister Scarecrow," said Jennifer, "you'll never be so lonesome again." And he never was because any time he got sad, he remembered that Halloween night and how everybody in town had come to see the Jack-O-Lantern and how all the people had made lanterns of their own and how they made them every Halloween after that.

That's how Jennifer Witch became famous. That's why every single year she's named "Queen of the Scarecrow Ball." When the witches mount their broomsticks on Halloween, they almost smile at the Jack-O-Lanterns who have been put in the windows to frighten them away. They know that it was a spell of Jennifer's that made the first Jack-O-Lantern. They know there's nothing to be afraid of. And deep in their hearts they know that witches aren't so fierce. In fact, they've all learned to make onion soup. . .it's delicious!

Leonard Leopard finally realized that it's better to be friendly than fierce and that he could be both strong and gentle.

Leonard Leopard

Leonard Leopard was the fiercest animal in the whole forest. It was no wonder that everybody was afraid of him. When Leonard roared…and he roared very often…even the bears and lions shivered and the little animals like the chipmunks, squirrels and rabbits would run and hide. Yes, the roars of Leonard Leopard were mighty fierce. As a matter of fact, even his teeny, tiny growls could be heard all over the forest. It was easy to understand why Leonard didn't have any friends — everybody was too afraid to go near him.

All the other animals had wonderful times together. Every month at the Noah's Ark Theater, they put on a big show. Everybody, just everybody, came to see it…everybody, that is, except Leonard Leopard. And he was not even invited. The other animals just hoped he wouldn't roar in the middle of the program. Nobody wanted to hear that. Why, even a little growl could have ruined the McSquirrel sisters' song. And they were the best singers in the forest. They had even been on television. The audience clapped and clapped and asked them to sing song after song. That is, they usually did. But on this particular night, the McSquirrel sisters hadn't even finished the first line when everybody rushed out of the theater.

And no wonder…because onto the stage pranced Leonard Leopard himself! When he got right smack in the middle, he let out such a roar that even the bears and lions decided to hide. "Stop this nonsense," said Leonard. "This singing is disturbing my rest." But Leonard didn't need to say anything…there wasn't a single, solitary soul left to talk to.

Yes, Leonard Leopard was fierce all right. That's why Rudy Rabbit just froze in his tracks the afternoon he turned around and saw Leonard standing beside him. Rudy tried to run away, but he couldn't move. After starting three times, the little rabbit finally squeaked, "Hello," and imagine his amazement when Leonard whispered back, "Go away." It wasn't a roar, mind you, or even a growl, it was a whisper. The little rabbit was surprised. He said, "What's the matter, Mr. Leopard?" And the leopard whispered back, "My roar, my roar, I've lost my roar. I don't know what to do." Without even thinking, Rudy said, "Come home with me. My mother will give you some medicine."

And Mrs. Rabbit did just that. She gave Leonard Leopard some honey cough medicine and a glass of hot lemonade. Then she said, "Now, Leonard, you come back here every hour on the half-hour and I'll give you more medicine. Now, don't worry. You will get your roar back...we'll see to that." "But you don't like my roar," whispered Leonard. "Of course I don't," said Mrs. Rabbit, "but it's a free forest and you're entitled to roar if you want to."

Well, Leonard did as he was told. Every hour on the half-hour, he came back to take his honey cough syrup and hot lemonade, and it was a funny thing...the little animals weren't at all afraid of a whispering leopard. In fact, they all waited outside Mrs. Rabbit's house to say hello to him and to hear him whisper back. But one afternoon after Leonard had had an especially large spoonful of honey cough syrup and an especially hot glass of lemonade, he said, "Hello," just as loud and clear as anyone. The little animals quivered and shook and shook and quivered. They expected Leonard to roar any minute, and they were too afraid to run.

But a strange thing happened. Leonard Leopard didn't roar...not then or ever, because, you see, Leonard had discovered that it was much more fun to have people say hello to him than it was to frighten them. And you wouldn't know that Leopard today. He's been the star of every show at the Noah's Ark Theater. He sings, he dances, he even plays the ukelele...and there's some talk that he may have a television program of his own — "Leonard Leopard and His Friends" — and that will probably include everybody in the whole forest because everybody likes Leonard Leopard...just everybody!

Robbie Rooster learned that friends are more valuable than fame and fortune and that real friends are there in good times and bad.

Robbie Rooster

It was said by authorities the world over that Robbie Rooster of Sunny Acres Farm had the finest crow in all Roosterdom. As soon as the sun peeked over the hill, he started his cock-a-doodle-doo. He woke Sunny Acres, the two neighboring farms and if the day was clear, he even wakened the town folk. Yes, the authorities agreed that Robbie Rooster had something to crow about.

Then came the day when Robbie decided that he was wasting his time. He didn't belong on a farm waking people up. . .he was meant to be a singer. So Robbie started to take lessons. Morning, noon and night, the farm echoed with his crow. . .always practicing the scale.

Finally, Robbie decided he was ready to go to the city. He didn't even take time to say goodbye to his nearest and dearest friends. The next thing they knew, he had his own television show, "Wake Up and Crow," sponsored by a chicken feed company. Robbie was a star. Everybody knew him, and when he crowed in the morning, he woke people all over the country. Yes, Robbie was a success.

But Robbie sang too much. He worked too hard and played too hard, and one morning, he discovered he couldn't crow above a whisper. The doctor put him to bed and said sadly, "Robbie, you may never sing again. There's nothing for you to do but go back to the farm." "They might not want me to come back," whispered Robbie. "I didn't even say goodbye." "Nonsense," said the doctor, "of course they'll want you to come back. They're your friends."

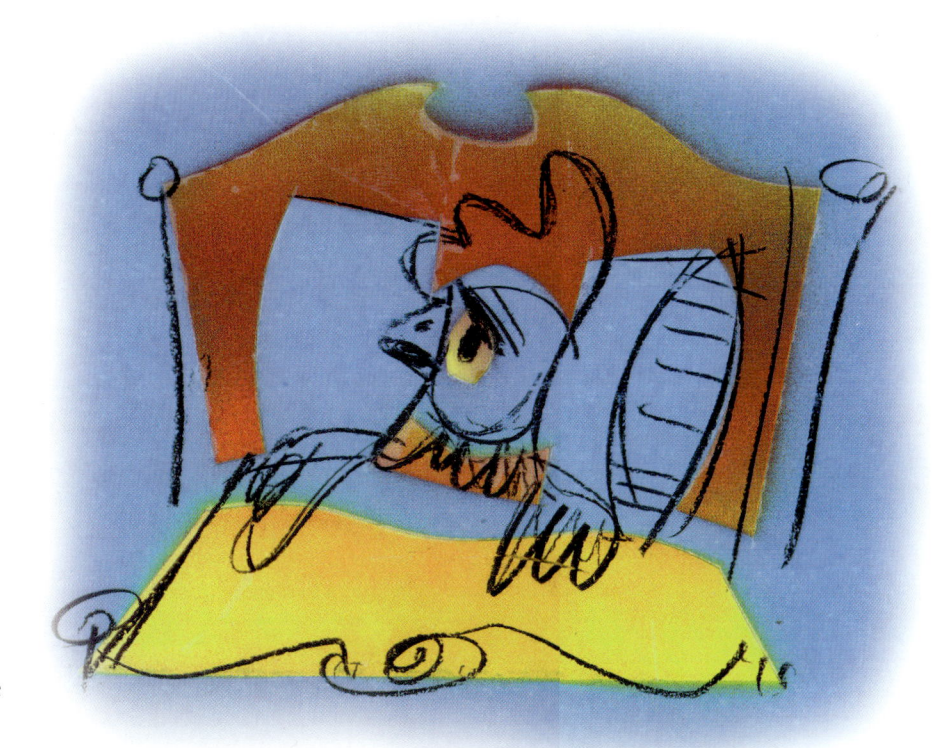

And the doctor was right. It was David Duckling who first saw Robbie. He rushed to meet him… "Robbie, Robbie Rooster, you're a sight for sore eyes, and I'm sure your crow will be a sound for lonesome ears." Robbie whispered, "I've lost my crow. I can't crow a note. I guess I'd better move on." "Don't be silly," said David. "You don't need a loud voice for visiting and you don't need to talk at all during checker games. We've missed you. Don't go away."

Robbie did stay at Sunny Acres. His voice came back and once again he woke Sunny Acres, the two neighboring farms, and once again on clear days the town folk heard him. But Robbie decided not to go back to the city. He didn't want to be a star except in the annual Barn Yard Follies. So if you happen to be near Sunny Acres Farm next summer, I hope you'll see the show. Robbie Rooster will sing the songs that made him famous, but he'll do his best when he crows his final number, "There's No Place Like Home." That's a song he crows from his heart.

The simplest things are sometimes the most valuable and love is the most important gift of all.

Dolly Dandelion

This story takes place in a flower garden. A very beautiful garden. There were roses and daffodils and tulips and pansies, just every kind of flower imaginable. And every single one of them was a champion. Every one of them had sent representatives to the State Fair, and every one of those representatives had come back with blue ribbons. Yes, indeed, this was a championship garden, and people came from miles around to see it. And every one of the visitors said the same thing.

"What a beautiful garden! What happy flowers!" And the flowers would smile and wave. But there was one flower who wasn't happy, and that was Dolly Dandelion. She didn't live in the garden, not really and truly. She lived just at the edge of the flagstone path. She could look in at the other flowers, but she couldn't go to visit them. In fact, the other flowers only nodded a very cold hello when Dolly said good morning. And Dolly Dandelion had never been to the State Fair. She had asked the committee if she could go. She had even said, "Please," but the chairman, Mathilda Rose, had told Dolly in no uncertain terms that she very definitely could not go to the fair. "In fact," said Mathilda Rose, "dandelions are not even flowers. They're weeds, and whoever heard of a weed going to the State Fair?" That did it! From that day on, Dolly Dandelion was the saddest creature you ever saw in your whole life.

She wouldn't even hold up her head. She didn't say good morning to anybody. All day long, she cried and cried. Finally one day, she heard a voice saying, "Dolly Dandelion, whatever is the matter with you?" "I'm unhappy," said Dolly. "That's what's the matter. And who are you, anyway, to bother me?"

"Who am I indeed," said the voice. "Just look at me and you'll see. I'm Peter Pixie, and I'm in charge of keeping flowers happy."

"I'm not even a flower," said Dolly. "I'm a weed. Everybody knows that."

"Now, Dolly, don't be silly," said Peter Pixie.

"I'm not being silly," said Dolly. "I wish I were a flower and I wish I were beautiful. That's what I wish."

"You're both of those," said Peter Pixie, "and I'll prove it to you. Here comes a little boy and his mother. Just listen to what he says."

And down the path came Jeffrey, the little boy who lived in the big house at the end of the flagstones. When he got near Dolly he said, "Look, Mother, dandelions. I like those flowers the very best of all, because when I see them, I know it's spring." Then he stopped and stooped over and picked Dolly up. "Here, Mother," said Jeffrey. "This is for you, because I love you."

Jeffrey's mother took Dolly in her hand and said, "Thank you, Jeffrey, this is the most beautiful flower in all the world."

And then, Dolly Dandelion knew that Peter Pixie had spoken the truth. She was sure of it when Jeffrey's mother put her in a vase and put her on the dining room table. To a little boy, she had meant spring, and because that little boy had given the flower to his mother with love, his mother had thought the flower beautiful. And if you mean spring and love, it doesn't make any difference if you can't go to the State Fair. Just making somebody smile is better than a blue ribbon. Better even than living in a championship garden. Dolly Dandelion was really, truly happy.

48

Two generations used the Magic Key. The legacy is still alive.
- Rosemary Conte Grosso

I watched the very first "Magic Toy Shop." It's still part of my life.
- Carol Holstein Killian

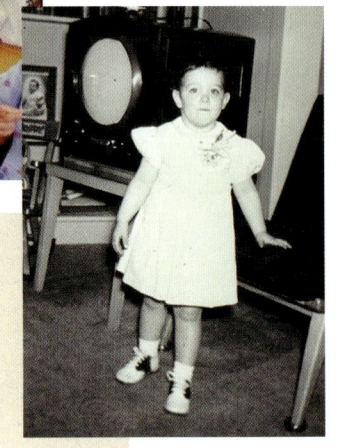

Mary Jo Romeo Barnello

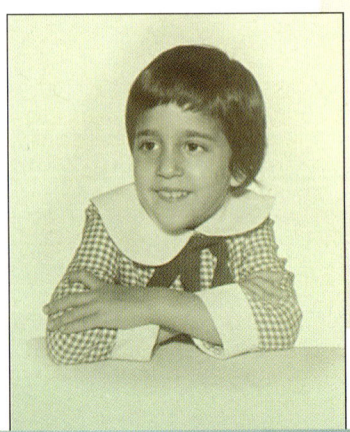

From all of us at "Magic Toy Shop," Thanks for remembering.

At the OHA, my children will relive my childhood.
- Mary Jo Romeo Barnello

I loved the show when I was 4, found it still magic at 14, and now best of all I share memories with John-Henry.
- Heather Harvey Lane